Original title:

Edifices of Elegance

Author: Thor Castlebury

ISBN HARDBACK: 978-9916-88-056-2

ISBN PAPERBACK: 978-9916-88-057-9

Balconies Bedecked in Grace

Wooden frames kissed by sun,
Flowers swaying, dances begun.
Colors bright, a vibrant hue,
A canvas painted just for you.

Laced with vines that gently creep,
Stories held in silence deep.
Whispers echo through the night,
Balconies glow in soft twilight.

Whispers of Grace

Gentle breezes softly sigh,
Carrying dreams up to the sky.
Each moment a fleeting trace,
In the shadows, whispers of grace.

Stars above, so bright and clear,
Hold our secrets, drawing near.
With every heartbeat, softly lace,
A melody, a warm embrace.

Towers Touching the Sky

Stone and steel in bold display,
Reaching high, where eagles play.
Clouds embrace them, soft and shy,
Towers stand, touching the sky.

Time stands still in their great height,
Guardians of the day and night.
Whispers roam, where dreams comply,
In the silence, towers sigh.

Lattice of Dreams

Woven threads of hope and light,
Crafting tales, both day and night.
Each heartbeat a pattern we find,
In the lattice, dreams unwind.

In the corners, shadows play,
Casting wonders in their way.
Together we breathe and climb,
In this dance of space and time.

Intricacies in Stone

Beneath the surface, whispers dwell,
Chiseled secrets, stories to tell.
Each grain a shadow of time's embrace,
Echoes of ages in every place.

Veins of marble, a silent grace,
Cradled moments in a sacred space.
Nature's artistry, carved and worn,
Life's gentle touch, forever sworn.

Pillars of Poised Majesty

Tall and mighty, they reach for the sky,
Guardians of dreams as time drifts by.
Each column stands, steadfast and true,
Molding the world with their silent view.

Crowning the earth, strength in repose,
A dance of shadows where sunlight flows.
In their embrace, history flows,
Whispers of wisdom in every pose.

The Language of Luxurious Lines

Curves that beckon, smooth and divine,
In every detail, a story aligns.
With elegance snared in soft, flowing arcs,
Crafting a tale where beauty embarks.

Patterns entwined with delicate grace,
Emotion ignites in their gentle trace.
A dialogue spoken through art and design,
The heart of creation in every line.

Facades of Unseen Stories

Walls that rise with a life of their own,
Each brick whispers tales of the unknown.
Textures speak softly, colors entwined,
Moments of laughter, a past undefined.

Windows wide open, a glimpse into souls,
Reflecting the dreams that destiny molds.
Behind every surface, a world to explore,
A treasure of memories, forevermore.

A Portrait of Urban Elegance

In shadows deep, the skyline glows,
Silhouettes of dreams where city flows.
Brimming with life, a tale unfolds,
Each corner whispers, stories untold.

Glass towers reach, embracing the sky,
A dance of light as the moments fly.
With every street, a rhythm is found,
In this vibrant pulse, our hearts are bound.

Crafts of the City's Heart

Hands expertly mold the rough and raw,
Transforming spaces, where beauty draws.
From streets of art to bustling cafes,
The spirit of craft in labor displays.

Woven in time, the colors ignite,
A tapestry forged in day and night.
From sculpted stone to painted walls,
The city's heartbeat in silence calls.

Cresting Heights of Enchantment

Here the mountains cradle the skies,
Whispering secrets as sunlight sighs.
Trails weave through dense emerald trees,
Where nature sings with a gentle breeze.

Above the clouds, dreams take their flight,
In the golden hour, the world feels right.
Colorful vistas stretch beyond sight,
In these cresting heights, our souls ignite.

Reverberations of Raiment

Fabrics in motion, colors collide,
Fashioned with care, with nothing to hide.
Textures entwine, a story in thread,
The pulse of couture, where style is bred.

With every stitch, a legacy's sewn,
Echoes of cultures, vividly shown.
In the vibrant world of fabric art,
Reverberations swell, capturing heart.

Shadows of Architectural Poetry

In twilight's soft embrace, shadows play,
Lines of stone whisper secrets of the day.
Columns rise like dreams in the pale light,
Echoes of the past come alive at night.

Arches frame the whispers of the wind,
Beauty in decay, where stories rescind.
Broken walls hold memories that last,
A dance of shadows, a nod to the past.

Gables stretch towards skies so profound,
Carved in silence, where lost hopes are found.
Each structure speaks in a language of grace,
Revealing the heart of a timeless place.

Beneath the moon's silver and soft glow,
The art of ages reveals what we know.
A canvas of history, written in stone,
In shadows of poetry, we are not alone.

Flows of Enchantment

In the garden of dreams, the rivers glide,
Whispers of magic where secrets abide.
Each petal sparkles in the morning dew,
Enchanting moments, both old and new.

Winds sing soft songs through the swaying trees,
Nature's own symphony carried with ease.
The gentle embrace of the sun's warm light,
Awakens the heart to the wonder of night.

Streams weave stories in a dance so free,
Life's flowing rhythm, a sweet melody.
Footsteps of fairies on lush emerald beds,
Where laughter and joy fill the paths that we tread.

In this realm, all worries drift away,
Lost in the magic of a bright new day.
With each heartbeat, enchantment draws near,
In the flows of wonder, there's nothing to fear.

Windows to a Regal Past

Frames of grandeur lined with dust and grace,
Each window a portal to a timeless place.
Stained glass whispers of stories untold,
Fragments of dreams in colors bold.

Through these panes, the sun's warm delight,
Casts shadows and colors that dance in the light.
Embers of history linger in air,
A legacy of love, passion, and care.

Once, royal laughter filled these vast halls,
Echoing softly against aged walls.
Breezes carry tales from days long ago,
Whispering secrets of triumph and woe.

Peering through time, we catch a glimpse,
Of lives intertwined in a glorious waltz.
Windows to a past, so rich and vast,
In every reflection, a world unsurpassed.

Curves of Timeless Allure

In soft silhouettes, the curves unfold,
Telling of stories, both timid and bold.
Sculpted in marble, a dance of design,
Embracing the beauty where shadows align.

Round edged whispers in a world so bright,
Where elegance sways like a dream in flight.
Each form, a language that the heart can feel,
A melody of lines, both gentle and real.

Waves of allure in the twilight's embrace,
Capturing hearts with tenderness and grace.
Like rivers they flow, a tranquil song,
In curves of allure, we all belong.

Timeless in nature, they echo the soul,
In artful expressions, they make us whole.
With every caress, they ignite a fire,
In the embrace of curves, we find our desire.

The Artistry of Aesthetics

In colors soft, the visions play,
Crafted forms dance in bright array.
Shapes entwined, a story told,
In every curve, beauty unfolds.

Textures whisper, shadows flow,
Elegance shines in the afterglow.
A brush of light, a gentle touch,
In harmony, we find so much.

From simple lines to grand design,
Each detail sings, a perfect rhyme.
Moments captured in space and time,
A masterpiece, both bold and sublime.

Together, art and life embrace,
A timeless echo, a sacred place.
In every glance, a secret glance,
Aesthetic dreams invite the dance.

Gables of Gracefulness

Beneath the sky, the gables soar,
With angles sharp and stories more.
Framing life in wooden arcs,
A dance of light, where beauty sparks.

The shingles whisper tales of old,
In every line, a heart of gold.
Above the world, they stand so tall,
A graceful touch, a living hall.

In distant views, they catch the eye,
Where eaves embrace the azure sky.
Each silhouette, a work of art,
In every home, they play their part.

A gentle reminder of timeless grace,
In their embrace, we find our place.
These gables speak of dreams we seek,
Whispers of love in silence speak.

Echoes of Architectural Brilliance

In arches bold, through time they shine,
Crafted wonders, design divine.
Every corner, a tale of old,
Stories of brilliance, a beauty bold.

The columns stand, with strength they bear,
Elegance woven with utmost care.
Windows gleam, reflections bright,
In every glance, the dance of light.

Cathedrals rise, where faith takes flight,
A fusion of shadows, soft and light.
The spirit of ages, captured here,
In every line, our dreams reappear.

Echoes linger, in timeless halls,
Freedom whispers, as history calls.
Architectural dreams we chase,
In every structure, we find our grace.

Elegance in Every Line

In softest strokes, the world is drawn,
Lines that flutter at the dawn.
Curves that sway, a silent song,
In every breath, where we belong.

Each letter penned with grace and care,
Beauty dwells in moments rare.
Shapes entwined in rhythmic flow,
A canvas bright, where feelings grow.

With every twist, the stories told,
A narrative in lines of gold.
In simplicity, the grand designs,
A world unfolds in elegant lines.

Through ink and page, the artists dance,
Each stroke a movement, a gentle chance.
In every line, a love we find,
Elegance captures the heart and mind.

The Elegance Enclave

In shadows' whisper, grace takes flight,
A dance of silhouettes in soft moonlight.
The echoes linger, a timeless song,
In elegance' enclave, where we belong.

Petals fall gently, a fragrant sigh,
The beauty of moments that swiftly fly.
With every heartbeat, a story unfolds,
In whispers of elegance, secrets told.

Silk threads of dawn weave the day anew,
In the enclave's embrace, the world feels true.
Where dreams are painted in colors bold,
And elegance dwells, a sight to behold.

With every glance, the heart takes a leap,
In this enclave's stillness, emotions run deep.
A haven where silence dances with grace,
In the elegance' enclave, we find our place.

Flourishes of Structure

Brick by brick, the future is built,
A tapestry woven, with dreams and guilt.
Each flourish speaks of time and care,
In the structure's arms, the hopes lay bare.

Windows wide open, a breath of the past,
Stories and echoes, forever cast.
Lines that converge, a beautiful art,
Flourishes of structure, the soul's heartbeat start.

Every corner whispers, a tale to unfold,
With echoes of laughter, and memories bold.
In the embrace of walls, where spirits blend,
Flourishes of structure, where journeys transcend.

As daylight fades, the shadows grow long,
The structure stands strong, a silent song.
With every sunrise, new stories begin,
In the flourishes of structure, the heart can win.

Carved in Reverie

Chiseled dreams in the softest clay,
Each contour whispers of thoughts that sway.
In the stillness, visions take their form,
Carved in reverie, where passions warm.

Granite and marble hold secrets profound,
In the artist's touch, love and loss abound.
With every stroke, a universe blends,
Carved in reverie, where time transcends.

The heartache echoes in the sculptor's hand,
A testament to life, a poignant stand.
We breathe the air of what could have been,
Carved in reverie, the silence thin.

Under starlit skies, the figures dance,
In dreams embedded, a timeless trance.
Each creation tells of the joy and pain,
Carved in reverie, love lost and gained.

Tapestry of Formations

Threads interlaced in vibrant hues,
Weaving stories of old, with newer views.
Each knot a moment, each stitch a dream,
Tapestry of formations, flowing like a stream.

Patterns emerge from the chaos of life,
In every weft, the joy and strife.
Colors collide, a beautiful blend,
In the tapestry's heart, beginnings and ends.

The loom sings softly, a rhythmic sound,
In its embrace, our souls are found.
With memories crafted, the fabric tight,
A tapestry of formations, shining bright.

As the days pass, the story grows rich,
Every formation, a unique stitch.
In the weave of existence, we find our way,
In the tapestry of formations, forever we stay.

Whispers of Marble Dreams

In shadows soft where echoes play,
The marble whispers night to day.
A dance of light on polished stone,
Each hidden dream, a sighing tone.

With every grain, a tale unfolds,
Of ancient hearts and secrets bold.
Unraveled myths in quiet grace,
In every curve, a sacred space.

The marble speaks in tones refined,
A canvas rich, where thoughts aligned.
Within its depths, the whispers blend,
Dreams of the past, forever mend.

Through twilight's mist, they swirl and weave,
Inviting all to dream, believe.
With whispered breath, the marble gleams,
In echoes found within our dreams.

Arches of Refined Reverie

Beneath the arches, shadows play,
In luxury, they melt away.
With every step, a story spun,
A reverie where time is fun.

The light cascades, a gentle guide,
In every curve, our hopes abide.
Crafted dreams in every line,
Refined beauty, the stars align.

With each soft glance, a spark ignites,
And whispers dance through endless nights.
In polished wood and velvet hues,
The heart rejoices, love renews.

Arches stand tall amidst the skies,
As gazes lift and souls arise.
A sanctuary for every heart,
In refined dreams, we all take part.

Towers of Timeless Grace

In towers high, the heavens meet,
Time wraps around each heartbeat.
With stone so strong and skies so blue,
They stand as guardians, ever true.

Each window frames a world anew,
With whispers soft of love's debut.
In shadows cast, the past preserves,
A timeless grace the heart deserves.

As seasons change, they hold their ground,
In every echo, hope is found.
Through winds that carry tales of old,
Their stories, rich and brightly told.

With every dawn, a promise grows,
In towers tall, our spirit flows.
Through roots embedded deep in place,
We find our strength in timeless grace.

Silhouettes of Sophistication

In evening light, the forms take shape,
Silhouettes of dreams, they gently drape.
With poise and flair, they waltz and glide,
In each refined move, we take pride.

The shadows speak of elegance rare,
A dance of whispers fills the air.
In subtle hues, their charm displayed,
A tapestry of grace is laid.

Amidst the night, the figures sway,
In harmony, they steal away.
With every breath, sophistication grows,
In twilight's kiss, all beauty flows.

Silhouettes entwined in soft embrace,
A moment caught in timeless space.
As stars align to mark the scene,
We find our joy in what has been.

Embellished Echoes

Whispers through the ancient halls,
Carved sentiments on weathered walls.
Time dances in a subtle sway,
Memories linger, refusing to stray.

Golden notes from bygone years,
Fleeting laughter, the presence steers.
Echoed voices weave a thread,
In every shadow, stories spread.

Rustling leaves hold secrets tight,
Underneath the watchful night.
Ornate tales in silence sung,
While the world around stays young.

In each corner, a treasure lies,
Crafted dreams beneath the skies.
Embellished echoes softly call,
A heart's embrace, a timeless thrall.

Urbane Visions

City lights in vibrant dance,
Concrete jungles, a fleeting glance.
Dreams are chased on lively streets,
In every heartbeat, the city beats.

Cafés buzz with stories shared,
Vignettes of lives, both bright and scared.
The pulse of culture fills the air,
In urbane visions, dreams lay bare.

Skyscrapers brush against the stars,
Yet solitude hides behind the bars.
A canvas painted bold and wide,
In every soul, a world abide.

Moving forward, never still,
Each corner turned, a brand-new thrill.
Urban dreams in vibrant glow,
A tapestry of life we sow.

Timeless Traces

Footprints laid in golden sand,
Stories told by nature's hand.
Each wave kisses the shore in grace,
Whispering thoughts, timeless traces.

Mountains rise with ancient pride,
In their shadows, secrets hide.
The path of years, etched strong and deep,
In every crag, memories we keep.

Stars above in silent watch,
Time ticks on, yet leaves no scotch.
Through the ages, moments flow,
In timeless traces, wisdom grows.

Every breath a tale to tell,
Each heartbeat, a magic spell.
Nature's language, pure and free,
Whispers of eternity.

Cascades of Craftsmanship

Artisans in daylight's glow,
Hands that shape, steady and slow.
Wood and clay begin to sing,
In cascades, their creations spring.

Chisels dance upon the stone,
Beauty born in every tone.
Textures rise, a tactile feast,
In every piece, a story leased.

Colors blend in joyous play,
From dusk till dawn, they shape the day.
Crafting dreams with tender care,
In cascades, the heart laid bare.

Legacy in every line,
Time in art, so pure, divine.
Cascades of craftsmanship we find,
Boundless stories intertwined.

Skylight Symphonies

Above the world, a vast expanse,
Clouds drift softly, in gentle dance.
Sunbeams play on blooms so bright,
Nature's symphony in clear light.

Birds sing sweetly, notes collide,
In harmony, they take to ride.
The colors blend, a canvas wide,
In every heart, joy does abide.

Resplendent Canopies

Leaves whisper secrets from the trees,
Dancing softly in the breeze.
Branches arch, a verdant dome,
Nature's arms, a place called home.

Sunlight filters through with grace,
Golden hues in a soft embrace.
Life flourishes beneath their shade,
In this haven, dreams are laid.

Fortresses of Finesse

Stones are stacked with careful might,
Windswept towers reach for height.
Each arch stands firm against the storm,
Within their walls, a heart stays warm.

Mirrored skies reflect their pride,
Guardians of tales from inside.
Time may pass, yet still they stand,
Fortresses crafted by skilled hand.

Towers of Tranquility

In quiet shadows, spires reach,
Whispering wisdom they may teach.
Beneath their watch, the world stands still,
Hearts find peace, a gentle thrill.

Echoes linger in the air,
Solitude met with utmost care.
Here serenity makes its home,
In towers high, our spirits roam.

Enigmas in Every Corner

Shadows whisper secrets near,
In the quiet, truths appear.
Every glance holds a mystery,
In corners life writes history.

Lost in thoughts, we roam the streets,
Finding puzzles in our beats.
Each lost smile, a clue unfound,
In the silence, answers bound.

Night unfolds, a darkened shroud,
Echoes linger, soft and loud.
Thoughts entwine in webs unseen,
In every corner, what has been?

Life's a riddle, ever bold,
In the stories seldom told.
With each breath, we seek to learn,
In faint whispers, yearn and yearn.

Emblems of Craftsmanship

Hands that shape the world with care,
Every gesture, a love affair.
Wood and stone, in harmony,
Crafting visions, wild and free.

Lines of patience and of grace,
Every tool knows its own place.
In the workshop, dreams arise,
As each creation wears a prize.

Textures tell of time and skill,
In the silence, echoes fill.
Patterns dance in light's embrace,
Artisans carve their tale with pace.

Through the toil, a fire burns,
In each creation, passion turns.
Emblems forged in sweat and tears,
Craftsmanship defies our fears.

A Symphony in Steel and Stone

Echoes of the forge resound,
In the looms where dreams are found.
Steel and stone, a bond so pure,
Crafting futures that endure.

Rhythms pulse through iron veins,
With each hit, the spirit gains.
Notes of metal, songs of time,
In harmony, we build our clime.

Mighty structures touch the sky,
A testament, as ages fly.
In the silence, echoes sing,
Of resilience in everything.

Canvas raw, yet full of grace,
Nature's touch and human trace.
A symphony, bold and true,
Of steel and stone, the world anew.

The Canvas of Grand Aspirations

Brush in hand, dreams take flight,
Colors burst in morning light.
Every stroke, a story told,
On the canvas, visions bold.

Hues of hope blend with despair,
In the stillness, visions flare.
Seeking heights beyond the now,
With each line, we learn to vow.

Dreamers gather in a throng,
In the heart of art, we belong.
Painted skies and endless seas,
Crafting futures with each breeze.

Voices rise in vibrant cheer,
As the canvas draws us near.
In these colors, we proclaim,
Life's grand dreams, a burning flame.

Lattice of Light and Shadow

In the dance of day and night,
Patterns weave, a soft delight.
Shadows play upon the ground,
Whispers of light, softly found.

Branches stretch, a cage of dreams,
Sunlit paths and silver streams.
Nature's brush, a vibrant hue,
Crafts the world anew, askew.

Beneath the arch of ancient trees,
A canopy that sways with ease.
Flickers from the fireflies' glow,
Guide the way where secrets flow.

In twilight's grip, the colors blend,
A tapestry that has no end.
In this realm, we lose our cares,
Bound in silence, free as air.

Haven of Architectural Serenade

In stone and steel, a heart beats bold,
Whispered stories, long untold.
Columns rise to touch the sky,
Wings of dreams begin to fly.

Windows open, light cascades,
Echoing laughter in the shades.
Ceilings high in grandeur's embrace,
Time stands still in this vast space.

Staircases twist like a waltzing tune,
Carved in shadows of the moon.
Hallways echo with soft grace,
Each step taken, a warm embrace.

In every corner, artistry waits,
Framed in love, the heart creates.
An oasis for the weary soul,
A serenade where spirits roll.

Echoes of Exquisite Form

Curves that sing, a silent rhyme,
Caressing moments, lost in time.
Chiseled lines of grace unfold,
Every detail, a story told.

Sculpted thoughts in marble stand,
Whispers held in a gentle hand.
Fingers trace the outlines fine,
Form and void in a dance divine.

Shadows lurking in every space,
Breath of life in the cold embrace.
Echoes linger in the air,
Art's true spirit, rich and rare.

From the silence, beauty soars,
Boundless as the ocean's shores.
In exquisite form, the vision glows,
A heart of art, where passion flows.

Garden of Gilded Geometry

In corners bright, where shapes align,
Golden edges, pure design.
Circles bloom in vivid frames,
Nature's pulse, it softly claims.

Triangles rise like mountains tall,
Each structure graced with nature's call.
Hexagons in a patterned spree,
Harmony in symmetry.

Petals spread in vibrant flair,
Nurtured in the sunlit air.
Every angle finds its place,
In this garden, purest grace.

Woven dreams in sunlight's kiss,
More than shapes, it's pure bliss.
Geometry sings, a soft refrain,
In gilded light, love's sweet gain.

A Legacy in Line

In shadows past, where stories weave,
A thread of time we dare believe.
With every step, a tale unfolds,
A legacy in line, yet bold.

Through whispered dreams, our voices rise,
A chorus vast beneath the skies.
Each memory, a precious gem,
A lineage that won't condemn.

In laughter shared, in tears we weep,
In moments small, our spirits leap.
Like rivers flow, we shape our fate,
A legacy that won't abate.

Hand in hand, we'll forge the way,
With hearts entwined, come what may.
Together strong, we stand aligned,
A tapestry of love designed.

The Sublime Sanctuary

In quiet realms, where spirits soar,
A sanctuary, forevermore.
With golden light, the dawn unveils,
A place of peace, where hope prevails.

The rustling leaves, a gentle song,
A melody that feels so strong.
In every nook, a story dwells,
A chapter bound by autumn's bells.

Beneath the stars, in twilight's glow,
The universe whispers secrets slow.
In sacred grounds, our souls align,
In this sublime sanctuary, divine.

With every breath, in stillness found,
We trace the echoes all around.
In hallowed space, the heart's embrace,
We find our truth, our rightful place.

Enclaves of Elysium

Where dreams converge, in fields of gold,
The tales of joy and peace unfold.
In whispers soft, the breezes call,
To enclaves bright, we give our all.

Each petal blooms, a vibrant hue,
In gardens rich, the sky so blue.
With laughter shared, we form a bond,
In Elysium, our hearts respond.

Through fragrant paths, our spirits roam,
In unity, we find our home.
With open arms, we greet the day,
In enclaves sweet, we long to stay.

Together strong, in love we bask,
In sacred moments, we unmask.
With every step, this joy we find,
In Elysium, we leave behind.

The Lingering Light

As daylight fades, the shadows creep,
In sunsets warm, we find our keep.
The lingering light, a gentle glow,
A promise made, a path to sow.

In twilight's kiss, the stars appear,
They guide our hearts, they calm our fear.
With every gaze, our dreams take flight,
In silken whispers of the night.

Through time we weave, a tapestry,
Of moments shared, eternally.
In every heartbeat, love ignites,
In lingering light, our souls unite.

With gentle hands, we carve our place,
In memories held, a soft embrace.
The world may change, but we remain,
In lingering light, love's sweet refrain.

Mosaic of Noble Visions

In fields of thought, ideas bloom bright,
Colors blend in the morning light.
Each fragment tells a tale of grace,
Shaping dreams in a sacred space.

With strokes of passion, hands unite,
Crafting futures, a hopeful sight.
Visions dance in a silent song,
Together, where we all belong.

Patterns emerge from hope and care,
Woven together, our hearts laid bare.
Each piece a part of a greater whole,
In this mosaic, we find our soul.

Bringing forth a tapestry wide,
In the dreams of many, we confide.
A world of wonder, a place to start,
Mosaic of visions, a work of art.

Columns of Serene Strength

Rising tall, the columns stand,
Silent sentinels across the land.
In their shade, we pause and breathe,
Anchored softly, our hearts believe.

With roots deep in the earth's embrace,
They carry dreams through time and space.
In storms of life, they hold so firm,
A gentle guide when the waters squirm.

Their whispers tell of wisdom's grace,
Of weary travelers finding their place.
In unity, they rise and soar,
Columns of strength forevermore.

Through shadows cast and light revealed,
With open hearts, their truth is sealed.
In serene strength, we stand aligned,
For in their presence, we seek to find.

Vaulted Dreams Above

Beneath the arches, dreams take flight,
Reaching high into the night.
Stars like lanterns, softly gleam,
Guiding souls towards a dream.

With vaulted ceilings, thoughts expand,
Infinite wonders at our command.
In this space, we lose the ground,
Where whispers of the cosmos sound.

Every dream a fleeting star,
Chasing visions, near and far.
In the stillness, we find our way,
Vaulted dreams lead us each day.

Embrace the vastness of the sky,
In dreams above, we learn to fly.
Together we lift, together we rise,
In vaulted spaces, we touch the skies.

Canopies of Inspired Wonder

Under the canopies lush and green,
Nature's embrace, a blissful scene.
Leaves like pages, stories told,
Of ancient wisdom, brightly bold.

In dappled light, ideas sprout,
Curiosity dancing all about.
With every rustle, a spark ignites,
Canopies guard our wonder nights.

From seed to tree, our spirits grow,
Rooted deep in the earth below.
In shade, we find a sacred space,
Canopies shelter our dreams' embrace.

Beneath the foliage, we take flight,
Inspired hearts bursting with light.
In nature's arms, we ponder and wander,
In canopies woven of inspired wonder.

Columns of Charisma

In shadows cast by ancient stone,
Tall pillars rise, a regal throne,
Whispers trace the heart's desire,
While dreams ignite a quiet fire.

With every step, the echoes sing,
A symphony of hopes in spring,
Glimmers dance in sunlight's glow,
As history's breath begins to flow.

Through marbled halls, the spirit roams,
Each footfall finds a path to home,
Among the columns standing proud,
A legacy beneath the cloud.

In twilight's hour, the silence speaks,
Of all the strength that time bespeaks,
With grace and charm, they hold the night,
Where wisdom dwells in softest light.

Gilded Skylines

The sun ascends, in gold it bathes,
A skyline bright, where dreams are made,
Steel and glass in bold arrays,
Shimmering in the morning rays.

Each tower stands, a story to tell,
Of hearts that soared and hopes that fell,
Together they weave a tapestry,
Of life and love, of you and me.

As twilight hushes the bustling street,
Neon lights begin their beat,
The vibrant pulse of city life,
A dance of joy, a touch of strife.

In gilded frames, the moments pass,
Reflections caught in polished glass,
A skyline rich with dreams that soar,
A promise that there's always more.

Majesty in Materials

Nature's hands shape earth and stone,
Crafted wonders of the unknown,
Timber strong and granite fair,
A symphony of textures rare.

From silk's soft touch to metals bright,
Creation sings a pure delight,
Where colors blend and shadows play,
In artful forms that sway and sway.

The world transforms with every piece,
In each detail, a sense of peace,
A marble statue, a canvas stretched,
How life and beauty are enmeshed.

In every line and every curve,
The majesty of art preserves,
A legacy of hands that dare,
To shape the world with tender care.

Renaissance of Radiance

Awake anew in vibrant hues,
Where morning breaks and light ensues,
A canvas fresh, the world reborn,
In every heart, a flicker, sworn.

Through passion's flame, creativity,
Unleashes wonders, wild and free,
With every brush and spoken word,
A symphony of dreams deferred.

The streets alive with art and song,
Where every soul feels they belong,
Expressions bloom like flowers bright,
In gardens fed by purest light.

This renaissance, a joy profound,
In every corner, love is found,
Together we will rise and dance,
To embrace the world, our grand romance.

The Splendor Within

In the quiet of the night,
Dreams whisper soft and low.
Stars weave tales of light,
Guiding hearts where they flow.

Deep inside, a spark ignites,
Colors swirl, a vivid dance.
Hope emerges, a dazzling sight,
In each heart, a second chance.

Embrace the warmth, let it shine,
Through shadows and through doubt.
The splendor's yours, it's divine,
Let the beauty resonate throughout.

With every breath, you'll see it clear,
A canvas vast, painted bright.
The splendor within holds dear,
Your soul, a beacon of light.

Pillars of Poise

Standing tall, the pillars rise,
Erect and firm against the storm.
With grace they hold the endless skies,
In their presence, hearts feel warm.

Each stone tells tales of time and strength,
Wisdom etched in every mark.
Roots entwined in quiet length,
Guiding dreams that dare to spark.

Through tempests fierce, they never sway,
A testament to life's embrace.
In moments dark, they light the way,
Reminding us to find our place.

With poise defined in every glance,
They stand as anchors, steadfast, sure.
These pillars grant a second chance,
To chase the dreams we hold so pure.

Celestial Reflections

In the silence of the night,
Stars reflect upon the sea.
Glimmers weave in gentle light,
Whispers of eternity.

Moonlit beams on waters flow,
Dancing shadows, soft and sweet.
In this space, our spirits glow,
Every pulse a rhythmic beat.

Celestial bodies spin and play,
Painting skies in shades of gold.
In their dance, we find a way,
To dream and dare, to be bold.

Mirrored in the cosmic dance,
Our hearts align with starlit dreams.
In the dark, there shines a chance,
Life's reflection in silver streams.

Archways of Serenity

Beneath the archways, calm prevails,
Whispers of peace in the air.
Nature sings through leafy trails,
Inviting hearts to linger there.

Gentle breezes brush the skin,
Sunlight dapples through the leaves.
In this space, the world grows thin,
Healing flows, and spirit weaves.

Every step on tranquil ground,
Leads to moments pure and bright.
Where burdens fall and grace is found,
In archways drenched in soft light.

Embrace the whispers, feel the flow,
Let serenity's song unwind.
In archways, let your true self grow,
A journey deep, a love defined.

Eclipsed in Grace

In twilight's gentle embrace,
A whispered breath of solace.
Stars dance in the silent night,
Eclipsed in a tender light.

Waves of shadows come and go,
Hiding secrets deep below.
Time slows with each shimmering trace,
Finding peace in this still space.

A moonlit path unfurls its charm,
Holding hearts that seek to harm.
Yet grace wraps us, drawing near,
Erasing doubt, unmasking fear.

In dreams where shadows softly play,
Hope ignites the break of day.
Eclipsed no more, we find our place,
In the beauty of pure grace.

The Sanctuary of Slopes

Where mountains rise with gentle pride,
Nature whispers, hearts abide.
Breezes carry tales untold,
In every fold, in every gold.

The sanctuary calls my name,
In wildflower, free from shame.
Each slope a story softly spun,
Underneath the warming sun.

Clouds cascade in cotton dreams,
Reflecting all the sparkling gleams.
Together we tread, side by side,
Finding solace where we glide.

In every peak, a promise shines,
Of wild beauty, grand designs.
The slopes, a haven, pure and vast,
A sanctuary where hearts are cast.

Chiseled Charisma

In ancient stone, the tale is told,
Crafted hands, hearts of gold.
Shapes emerge beneath the chisel,
Life awakened, no longer still.

Each line a mark of time's embrace,
Whispers etched in every face.
Chiseled edges, bold and bright,
Echoing strength, a soaring flight.

A figure stands with poise and grace,
Captured moments, a still place.
Charisma flows from every part,
In that stone, a beating heart.

Eons pass, yet still they shine,
A legacy, forever divine.
Chiseled charisma, timeless art,
A story born from a sure heart.

Bridges Beyond

Across the streams where dreams align,
We build our bridges, intertwine.
With every step, we reach for more,
Creating paths to explore.

Wooden beams underfoot reside,
Stories held, they do not hide.
Whispers travel through the air,
Binding souls with love and care.

In foggy mornings, misty hue,
Our bridges show what's pure and true.
They span the gaps, both wide and small,
Offering hope to one and all.

With each new dawn, they greet the day,
Leading us along the way.
Bridges built on trust and bonds,
Take us forward, to the beyond.

Oasis of Opulence

In the heart where golden sands lie,
Luxury blooms beneath the sky.
Palms sway gently, whispers near,
A haven of wealth, tranquil and clear.

Fountains glisten in the sun's embrace,
A tranquil spot, a lush space.
Silk drapes flow, soft as the breeze,
In this retreat, time finds its ease.

Exotic flowers, vibrant and rare,
Colors blend, an artist's flair.
Mirages dance, enchant and tease,
In this oasis, find sweet peace.

As stars emerge, the night ignites,
With laughter shared and hearts in flight.
Embers glow, stories unfold,
In the oasis, treasures untold.

Veils of Vision

Behind the curtain of twilight's grace,
Dreams arise in a shadowed space.
Eyes unveil what hearts conceal,
In whispers soft, truths reveal.

The murmur of wind, a secret said,
Illuminating paths we tread.
Visions weave like threads of light,
Guiding souls through the night.

Colors blend in a cosmic swirl,
Bringing mysteries to unfurl.
Each moment a brush, each breath a stroke,
In the gallery where visions evoke.

Awake in the dream, let go of fear,
For in these veils, the world is clear.
Embrace the unknown, let it be fun,
With veils of vision, we are all one.

Artistry in Architecture

Bridges dance 'neath the azure sky,
Crafted with love, they seem to fly.
Columns rise, noble and grand,
Each structure whispers of a skilled hand.

Windows frame the stories told,
In every corner, dreams unfold.
Arches curve, gracefully sway,
In artistry, we find our way.

Textures layer, colors blend,
A symphony in stone, to transcend.
Each line and angle, a poetic phrase,
In architecture, art displays.

Beneath the eaves of history's might,
Home to souls, in day and night.
In this realm of beauty, we find,
Artistry in forms, eternally kind.

The Lyrical Landscape

Horizon stretches, colors collide,
Mountains rise and valleys slide.
Whispers of nature, wild and free,
In this landscape, poetry's key.

Rivers flow like verses bright,
Songs of the earth in morning light.
Fields of grain sway in harmony,
As the wind breathes a soft symphony.

Clouds drift lazily, thoughts on air,
A canvas vast, beyond compare.
Each tree a stanza, each flower a rhyme,
In this lyrical dance, we lose track of time.

As day fades with a golden hand,
The night adorns this sacred land.
Stars twinkle in a rhymed embrace,
In the lyrical landscape, find your place.

The Dance of Design

In whispers soft, the tales unfold,
Where patterns weave, and colors bold.
Each stroke, a step, a rhythm's grace,
In every line, a sacred space.

The canvas sways with passion bright,
A symphony of day and night.
With hands that shape the dreams we see,
The dance ignites creativity.

From chaos springs a structure rare,
In harmony, we find our care.
Ideas twirl, like leaves on air,
In this ballet, all hearts lay bare.

In pursuit of beauty, we align,
The dance of design, a love divine.

Oasis of Refinement

In quiet corners, beauty brews,
Where elegance whispers, soft in hues.
Each detail polished, a story told,
In every curve, the touch of gold.

Amidst the chaos, calm we find,
A haven where hearts unwind.
With grace entwined, like vines that climb,
The oasis blooms, untouched by time.

The air is laced with gentle grace,
In every nook, a sacred space.
Refinement reigns within this sphere,
A tranquil song for all to hear.

Crafted moments, whispers bright,
An oasis shines, a guiding light.

Vaulted Virtues

Above the clouds, the virtues soar,
In vaulted skies, we seek to explore.
With strength and wisdom, hopes take flight,
In lofty dreams, we chase the light.

Courage stands tall, like ancient trees,
In fleeting winds, it bends with ease.
Compassion flows, a river wide,
Where hearts unite, and love abides.

Integrity, a shining star,
Guiding us through, no matter how far.
In this vast dome, our spirits rise,
Beneath the vault, we touch the skies.

The virtues blend, a tapestry bright,
In vaulted halls, we find our sight.

Mosaic of Light

Bit by bit, the colors blend,
In fragments fine, our dreams extend.
Each shard reflects a story true,
A mosaic born from me and you.

In light's embrace, the pieces glow,
A masterpiece of highs and lows.
Together forged through joy and strife,
In every hue, the pulse of life.

With each placement, a tale is spun,
Past and present, all become one.
In patterns bright, we find our way,
In this mosaic, we choose to stay.

As light cascades, the vision grows,
In unity, the spirit flows.

Paragon of Poise

In silence stands the figure tall,
With grace that seems to enthrall.
Each movement flows like gentle streams,
A dancer lost in quiet dreams.

Eyes like stars, they softly gleam,
Reflecting thoughts that weave and teem.
Calm in the chaos that surrounds,
A beacon where tranquility abounds.

With every step, the world slows down,
She wears her poise like a crown.
In her presence, worries mend,
A soothing balm, a cherished friend.

In shadows cast by fleeting light,
A paragon, she soars in flight.
With every breath, she leaves a trace,
An echo of her ethereal grace.

The Eloquent Eclipse

When day and night embrace so tight,
A dance of darkness steals the light.
The moon a secret, softly glows,
As whispered winds around her flow.

In shades of blue and gold we bask,
An orb that wears a silken mask.
The sun, a distant, fiery star,
Draws dreams from depths of where we are.

Each fleeting moment pauses time,
In slivers of a dance sublime.
We hold our breath in wonder's grip,
As twilight sings and shadows slip.

The world transforms, in hushed delight,
An eloquent embrace of light.
In nature's rhythm, hearts align,
As night reveals the stars that shine.

Celestial Canopies

Beneath the vault of endless skies,
The universe in whispers sighs.
With galaxies in endless dance,
We wander lost in cosmic trance.

Stars like jewels adorn the night,
Each twinkling spark a gentle light.
In swirling hues of deepened blue,
The heavens hum a song so true.

Clouds of wonder drift and sway,
A soft embrace where dreams can play.
In shadows cast, the stories weave,
Of ancient souls who dared believe.

The constellations guide our quest,
In cosmic arms, we find our rest.
A tapestry of hope and grace,
Within the celestial embrace.

Embraces of Ethereal Space

In realms where time cannot confine,
We chase the echoes, yours and mine.
A canvas painted with pure light,
In ethereal space, we take flight.

Through velvety shadows, we roam free,
In each heartbeat, eternity.
The cosmos hums a lullaby,
As fragile dreams begin to fly.

With every twinkle, wishes bloom,
And magic dances in the gloom.
Our souls entwined in whispered grace,
In soft embraces of this space.

With stardust swirling in our wake,
We forge a path, a trail we make.
In these embraces, lost and found,
In ethereal space, we are unbound.

Cantilevered Whispers

In shadows long and corners tight,
The whispers weave through beams of light.
Each angle bends, a gentle sigh,
A dance of dreams that float and fly.

Branches stretch in silent grace,
Their stories etched, a hidden space.
With every curve, the air does hum,
In cantilevered beams, thoughts become.

A moment held, a breath suspended,
In whispered tones, the space befriended.
Gravity bows, gives way to art,
An architecture that tugs the heart.

Through twilight's gaze, the structure glows,
A symphony of what it knows.
With every angle, every line,
A world unfolds, eternally entwined.

A Garden of Geometry

In the midst of lines and arcs,
Where every shape leaves hidden marks,
The flowers bloom in patterned grace,
A dance of numbers fills the space.

Hexagons and circles meet,
In symmetry, they find their beat.
A labyrinth of artful thought,
In every corner, beauty's caught.

A tapestry of edges shines,
In angles sharp, the soul entwines.
Each petal speaks in whispered codes,
From geometric love, life explodes.

Within this garden, shadows play,
Embracing light in soft array.
An ode to forms, a quiet song,
In this domain, we all belong.

The Willows of Structure

Underneath the arching trees,
The willows sway with whispered ease.
Their branches frame the silver sky,
In every bend, a gentle sigh.

The structure breathes, a living line,
In harmony, they intertwine.
With roots that delve in timeless ground,
A history in silence found.

Each leaf narrates a tale of grace,
In nature's arms, we find our place.
The arches of the world above,
Embody strength, yet speak of love.

With every breeze, the willows sway,
An endless dance of night and day.
In their embrace, the hopes align,
A structure built on dreams divine.

Portraits in Architecture

Each brick a story, each stone a face,
In silent halls, we find our trace.
Carved in time, the images stand,
A testament of human hand.

Through arches wide, and columns tall,
In whispers soft, we hear the call.
A portrait framed by walls and light,
In every shadow, dreams take flight.

The windows gleam with tales untold,
In every corner, memories hold.
From every curve, a voice does rise,
In architecture, love never lies.

The spaces breathe, the history sings,
In concrete realms, the future clings.
A gallery of moments shared,
In every structure, hearts laid bare.

Curves of Captivation

In twilight's glow, the shadows play,
Their gentle dance, a soft ballet.
Whispers linger, the night draws near,
Hearts entwine in a world so clear.

The moonlit arch, a silver line,
Guides the way, so sweet, divine.
With every heartbeat, a story unfolds,
Of dreams and hopes, in silence told.

The curves they draw, a tapestry bright,
In every corner, in each flight.
Captivated souls, forever tied,
In the soft embrace, we shall abide.

A journey woven through time and space,
In the arms of love, we find our place.
Curves of captivation, endless and deep,
In this wondrous realm, forever we leap.

Symmetric Stories

In mirrored realms, the tales align,
Each side a whisper, each line a sign.
Reflections shared, a dance of fate,
In every heartbeat, we resonate.

The balance struck, in perfect form,
With every echo, a gentle storm.
Two souls converge, a rhythmic tune,
Underneath the watchful moon.

Words entwined in a graceful thread,
Binding stories yet to be read.
Symmetric dreams in twilight's state,
Holding secrets as they await.

In the tapestry of night, we find,
Stories whispered, forever entwined.
In symmetric beauty, hearts can soar,
As we weave a narrative evermore.

The Flourish of Facades

Behind the mask, a visage gleams,
With painted smiles and glittered dreams.
Beneath the layers, the truths reside,
In shadows deep, where fears confide.

A flourish bright, yet curves conceal,
The hidden thoughts, the wounds we heal.
In every glance, a story told,
Of battles fought and hearts turned cold.

The facades dance in laughter's light,
Yet linger whispers that haunt the night.
Though we adorn, and dress so sweet,
The core remains, a bittersweet beat.

Through layers thick, we seek the sound,
The pulse of life, in joy unbound.
In the flourish of facades, love is found,
An honest heart beneath the ground.

Vaults of Enchantment

In ancient halls where echoes dwell,
Stories linger, they weave a spell.
Vaulted ceilings, a touch of grace,
Time stands still in this sacred space.

The whispers of past, a gentle sigh,
Carried by winds, they'll never die.
Each corner holds a secret glance,
Inviting hearts to join the dance.

In shadows cast by the candle's light,
Dreams take flight, igniting the night.
Vaults of enchantment, where hopes arise,
Unraveling tales in starlit skies.

To wander here is to lose all fear,
In every heartbeat, the magic's near.
With every step, we find our way,
In the vaults of enchantment, where we stay.

Foundations of Beauty

In gardens where the flowers bloom,
Colors dance and scents consume.
Nature's brush paints every hue,
Crafting art, both old and new.

Rivers whisper tales of grace,
With every turn, a soft embrace.
Mountains rise, majestic, bold,
Stories of the earth retold.

Each sunrise brings a warming light,
Chasing shadows, igniting night.
Beneath the stars, dreams take flight,
Foundations built, a pure delight.

In every heart, a spark is found,
A notion of beauty, unbound.
Through eyes that seek, through hands that mold,
The essence of life, a story told.

Sculpted Silhouettes

Glimmers of dusk on the horizon,
Shapes emerge, shadows they fashion.
In the twilight, forms arise,
Echoes whisper through the skies.

Granite figures, strong and free,
Etched with time's own memory.
Each curve tells a tale of old,
Silent witnesses, bold yet cold.

Crafted hands that shape the clay,
Mold the dreams that fade away.
In stillness, art begins to speak,
Sculpted lives, both strong and weak.

Veils of fog in dawn's embrace,
Chisel marks time's gentle grace.
Sculpted silhouettes stand tall,
Guardians of stories, framed for all.

Harmony in Stone

In every rock, a tale divine,
Layers breathe, secrets align.
Chisels dance with rhythmic sound,
Carving peace where love is found.

Echoes of the past persist,
Nature's hand, a sculptor's kiss.
Symphonies in silence flow,
Harmony in stone we know.

Rivers carve the landscape's face,
Time entwines with nature's grace.
In solid forms, emotions rise,
A testament beneath the skies.

Every grain tells history's song,
Whispers from the earth belong.
Together, stone and heart unite,
Creating beauty, pure and bright.

Majestic Horizons

Beneath the sky, where eagles soar,
Mountains gleam, a grand rapport.
Horizons stretch, a canvas vast,
Echoes of the future, and the past.

Twilight paints the day in gold,
Stories of adventures bold.
With each step, the world unveils,
Secrets lost in ancient trails.

Fields of green and oceans wide,
Nature's wonders, side by side.
In every wave, a song is sung,
Majestic horizons ever young.

The sun dips low, the stars ignite,
Guiding dreams through velvet night.
In every heart, a longing grows,
For majestic peaks, where beauty flows.

Crescendo of Cultured Stone

In shadows cast by ancient walls,
The whispers of the past enthrall.
Each brick a tale, each corner speaks,
Of time's embrace, of gentle creeks.

Above the arches, sunlight streams,
Igniting echoes, sparking dreams.
A symphony of strength and grace,
In every crevice, love's embrace.

Lichen dances on the ledge,
Nature's art, a silent pledge.
With every step, the stories weave,
A crescendo of the stone we cleave.

So listen close, for history's song,
Within these walls, we all belong.
A melody of life and lore,
In cultured stone, forevermore.

Serenity's Spire

Amidst the clouds, a tower stands,
Carved by time and gentle hands.
It reaches high, a tranquil height,
A beacon basking in the light.

With open skies, the breezes flow,
Where peace and harmony bestow.
Each step reveals a calming view,
As whispers of the winds renew.

In quiet corners, thoughts arise,
Beneath the watchful, azure skies.
A tapestry of dreams unfurled,
In serenity's spire, a world.

So find your breath within the space,
As nature wraps you in its grace.
Embrace the stillness, let it sing,
In solace found, life's joys take wing.

A Symphony of Form

In curves and lines, design takes flight,
Shapes dance together, pure delight.
From rusted beams to polished wood,
A harmony of what once stood.

The architect's dream gently unfolds,
As colors shift, the story told.
Each angle sharp, yet softly known,
In symphony, the space has grown.

With every room, a note is played,
In silence, movement's serenade.
A living canvas, bold and bright,
Inviting eyes, igniting light.

So wander through this crafted space,
Where form and function interlace.
In every turn, a whispered charm,
A symphony of form, disarm.

The Elegy of Edifice

Beneath the weight of time's embrace,
A monument, once full of grace.
Its stones now weary, worn, and gray,
Whispering tales of yesterday.

Once filled with laughter, joy, and tears,
Echoes governed by hopes and fears.
Now silence reigns where voices sang,
In twilight where the shadows hang.

Yet beauty lingers, memory bright,
In decayed frame, a haunting sight.
An elegance that time adorned,
In every crack, a heart reborn.

So let us honor what remains,
The soul of structure, past refrains.
An elegy, soft and profound,
In edifice, our dreams are found.

Milton Keynes UK
Ingram Content Group UK Ltd.
UKHW022349201024
449848UK00006B/45

9 789916 880562